THOMAS ADÈS

Three Studies from Couperin

for chamber orchestra

(2006)

I. Les amusemens
II. Les tours de passe-passe
III. L'âme-en-peine

FULL SCORE

© 2006 by Faber Music Ltd
This edition first published in 2022 by Faber Music Ltd
Bloomsbury House, 74–77 Great Russell Street, London WC1B 3DA
Music processed by Jeremy Hughes
Cover image from *Les Fêtes Galant* commissioned especially from Matthew Picton
Printed in England by Caligraving Ltd
All rights reserved

ISBN10: 0-571-53656-5
EAN13: 978-0-571-53656-6

Permission to perform this work in public must be obtained from the Society
duly controlling performing rights unless there is a current licence for public performance
from the Society in force in relation to the premises at which the performance is to take place.
Such permission must be obtained in the UK from Performing Right Society Ltd,
www.prsformusic.com

Three Studies from Couperin was commissioned by the Basel Chamber Orchestra,
kindly supported by Ernst von Siemens Musikstiftung
and Paul Sacher Foundation

The first performance was given by the Basel Chamber Orchestra,
conducted by Thomas Adès, at the Martinskirche, Basel, on 21 April 2006

Three Studies from Couperin is recorded by the Chamber Orchestra of Europe,
conducted by the composer, on EMI Classics 4578132 (CD)
and by the Norwegian Radio Orchestra, conducted by Andrew Manze,
on BIS-8003 (Digital download)

Duration: *c*.13 minutes

To buy Faber Music publications or to find out about the full range of titles available
please contact your local retailer or Faber Music sales enquiries:

Faber Music Limited, Burnt Mill, Elizabeth Way, Harlow, CM20 2HX, England
Tel: +44 (0) 1279 82 89 82
fabermusic.com

ORCHESTRA

flute 1 (doubling alto flute)
flute 2 (doubling bass flute)
clarinet in B♭ or A
bassoon

2 horns in F
trumpet in B♭

percussion (1 player):
    five-octave bass marimba, 2 small metal bars –
    or anvils (enclumes), bass drum, 3 timpani
    (large to small), 5 roto-toms (see below)

2 string orchestras (ideally 4.4.3.3.2 players each)

The score is in C
Orchestral parts available on hire from the publishers

SEATING ARRANGEMENT

The woodwind and brass players should be positioned in one line along the back of the orchestra. The percussionist should be placed centrally, behind them. String Orchestra I is on the conductor's left. String Orchestra II is on the conductor's right.

ROTO-TOMS

12 pitches are needed as follows:

N.B. These are sounding pitches, <u>never</u> an octave lower or higher.

The part has been arranged for 5 pedal roto-toms, or 5 hand-tuned roto-toms covering:

More drums can be used if available, to reduce the number of retunings. However, there must be at least two which are the smallest available size (less than or equal to 6"/15cm in diameter) in order to obtain the highest pitches which must be played as written (not an octave lower).

CONTENTS

I. Les amusemens *page* 1
II. Les tours de passe-passe *page* 31
III. L'âme-en-peine *page* 55

Three Studies from Couperin

I. Les amusemens

THOMAS ADÈS

* Wooden mutes if possible

Copyright © 2022 by Faber Music Ltd

* if pitch is clear enough, play harmonic; otherwise, ordinary note

Premier Couplet

* if pitch is clear enough, play harmonic; otherwise, ordinary note

Deuxième Rondeau

24

29

II. Les tours de passe-passe

III. L'âme-en-peine